21 Days to Feminine Magnetism

Your Guide to Getting #Wifedup

Angela S. Holcomb

Dedication

Thank you, God, for imparting this knowledge upon me! I felt scared and unqualified but here I am doing it anyway. Hopefully, my movement to help more women become wives is a burnt offering to you.

This book is dedicated to all the women out there who truly have been waiting for a book that will guide them on how to take back their feminine power in love! They have been patiently waiting on this book. They have given me motivation to put my knowledge to pen and paper. Some days I felt unsure about my creating this book, but those women kept me going. The will to help women realize who they really are propelled me to finish this book.

For anyone who comes across this book, I am excited that you are on a journey of discovering your feminine essence.

This is dedicated to all of you who inspired this book because of your desire for this information. I couldn't have done it without you.

CONTENTS

INTRODUCTION

"The first step toward change is awareness. The second step is acceptance."

-Nathaniel Branden

Congratulations on taking control of your love life. I am so excited you decided to embark on this journey. I am ecstatic for you! I am literally jumping out of my seat.

You purchased this book because you believe it will take you from where you are to where you want to be. I am incredibly proud of you for owning your shit and taking your love life to the next level. This book will 1000% change your life and get you closer to having the happily ever after you desire. You must keep an open mind, remove your ego and do the work. I repeat, you must do the work.

I want you to get prepared to be uncomfortable. What I am going to show you is nothing like anything you have learned about love and relationships before. Femininity will change your life. Over the next 21 days, you will grow into a feminine magnet who has men falling under her spell.

Who am I and why do I have expertise to tell you anything?

I do not have worldly credentials. I know that God put a message on my heart to share with women. I did not come up with this information on my own. My purpose is to help women understand that femininity is the key to unlocking everything you have desired in love. Being a feminine woman will inspire men to protect you, provide for you, profess their love for you and ultimately give you the commitment you are seeking.

I created this book so that women would have a hands-on guide that will help them get out of masculine energy and into feminine energy. Implementing what you learn in this book will forever change the game for you.

Society has programmed many women to believe that they need to work hard and earn the love and commitment of men.

However, this is not what men respond to in the long term.

Many women were taught to be strong, independent and to live without a man. Many women were not taught how to interact with men in a way that will have him begging to make you his. Many women were not taught how to tune into their feminine essence to helplessly attract men to them. Many women were not taught that they are worthy of being in a good relationship. Many women were not taught how to become a good partner. But you bought this book, so you will be miles ahead of those women.

My goal over the next 21 days is to help you tune into your feminine essence so that you can attract the highest quality, masculine man for you. I want you to experience how shifting your mindset, behaviors, beliefs and mannerisms from the masculine to the feminine will completely revolutionize your love journey.

It may sound farfetched, but trust me. If it worked for me,

it will work for you.

Getting the love and the commitment that you desire does not have to be difficult. Actually, it isn't hard at all. It is simple. If you stop doing what does not work and begin doing what does work, then you can achieve your dream relationship.

The only reason you do not have the relationship of your dreams with as high-quality masculine man is because you are not embracing your feminine core and you have limiting beliefs about what you deserve. In other words, femininity combined with a high self-worth is a force to be reckoned with in the dating world. Men will fall at your feet and work to win you.

Why should I become magnetically feminine?

Because femininity is what attracts the type of man you want. I will go into more detail as the guide progresses. Trust me, this is why most of your past relationships did not move forward; you were stuck in masculine energy. Masculine energy is the cause for a great deal of relationship issues unless you are dealing with a feminine man.

The only thing that is stopping you from progressing is YOU! Not him! Not your ex! Not the fuckboy from 2011...BUT YOU!

I used to be where you are. Struggling with the rejection from one man after another. I didn't feel like I deserved true love and commitment even though it was something I deeply desired. Then I stopped looking outside to what men were doing and to look within to what I was doing. I wanted to know what kept me stuck and a failure in love. And thus, I began my personal research and now I'm going to share it with you. Does that sound familiar? If yes, then this guide is definitely for you.

Over the next 21 days, I will be showing you how to embrace your feminine mystique. I will give you daily assignments to complete that will help you to reprogram your mindset toward your love life. Feel free to write in a notebook or elsewhere if you need more space.

I want to help women obtain their happily ever after's. Now, if you want to achieve this fairy tale with ease, stay 'til the end.

You may get excited and want to skip ahead: DO NOT! Take it one day at a time. Rome wasn't built in a day. It took you a lifetime to get into your current mindset and it will not be an overnight process to reprogram it, so be patient and follow the daily work.

The assignments should take no more than 15 minutes each day, a few days may take a bit longer. The time you are spending on this challenge are the seeds you are sowing for your future growth.

When I first learned how to embrace femininity I was confused, hesitant and lost. But as I put my ego to the side and began to practice femininity, I saw changes in the men I dated and within myself. I was more relaxed and poised. I did less and received more than I ever had before from men. I was sold!

I've coached clients who have stopped engaging in masculine energy and starting engaging in feminine energy and have seen dramatic changes in their men. A woman saw a long-time boyfriend of 8 years, talk marriage after working with me for 1 month! Prior, he dodged the topic like the plague. He even took her to look at rings!

I am so excited for you! Are you?

Before we start on Day One, I want to give you a few questions for you to contemplate. Take a few minutes to look inward to answer these questions honestly. This exercise will prepare you for the next 21 days.

Daily Assessment

1. Why did you buy this book?

____

____

____

____

____

2. Are you ready to shift your entire mindset surrounding love?

____

____

____

____

____

3. Are you open to keeping a roster? Are you open to dating multiple men at once?

4. On a scale of 1-10, how committed are you to transforming your love life over the next 21 days?

5. How will it feel to have men falling all over you? For it to be literally raining men?

____

____

6. What time of day do you commit to do this every day?

____

____

____

____

____

Additional Notes:

DAY

1

YOUR POLAR OPPOSITE

"None of us are just black and white, or never wrong and always right. No one exists without polarities." -Suzy Kassem

Polarity is science. Polarity is nature. If you pay attention to nature you will see that all things have their opposite, their complement. As the moon has the sun. As the light has the dark. As cold has hot. We live in a polar universe.

Human attraction is very scientific. It is based on the Law of Polarity. Polarity is magnetic. Polarity is attracting the complement of your energy. For example, if you are masculine, you will attract and vibe best with a feminine counterpart. If you are feminine, you will attract a masculine counterpart. This is how human sexual attraction works.

Relationships are all about two opposing energies coming together to balance each other out. The yin and yang. Yin is feminine and yang is masculine.

Sexual attraction goes beyond looks. You can be an attractive woman with "womanly" appearance and dress yet exude masculine energy. You are a man in women's attire. In these cases, masculine men are not able to balance their energy with you because you do not have feminine energy. This is why masculine women often get used for sex by masculine men. They cannot connect with you on the energetic level so they connect with you on the superficial level of lust. So, if you find yourself in a lot of friends with benefits situations, one-night stands, or situationships, you have been operating in masculine energy.

Since these energies repel each other they cannot produce a long-lasting connection. Think of the magnetism of two AA batteries. When you put them into a device you always put them in with + facing -. This is the only way they will work and produce power for your devices. This is the same concept with sexual attraction among the sexes. Femininity is negative and masculinity is positive. They "power" each other, so to speak. If you put any other combination together, your device will not work. A committed relationship is the 'device.'

You need to focus on your energy not your attractiveness. Do not get me wrong, you should definitely look your best by eating right and getting into shape in order to attract the highest quality of men. However, the physical has never kept a man. Masculine men stay with women because they exude a feminine vibe that he finds absolutely irresistible and he feels energized by her presence.

A masculine man wants a feminine woman because her presence makes him feel like a king. A masculine man needs to be the leader in the relationship in order to be happy. Masculine energy is about pursuing, overcoming, protecting, providing, and leading. When a man is allowed to show his masculinity to a woman he feels like he is her hero. She then feels safe, loved, and protected. Through this dynamic a beautiful relationship can blossom.

A masculine woman becomes his competition, not his companion. When she is masculine she becomes possessive, controlling, aggressive, pursuant and afraid of vulnerability. Polarity disappears. Vulnerability is what creates deep connection, attraction, and desire for a man.

Women who understand polarity and make it work for them have thriving lifelong commitments from men.

Women when they operate in masculine energy create severe

depolarization and demagnetization with masculine men. Polarity is more important than chemistry and having things in common in creating a lasting connection. As crazy as it sounds, it's true.

Polarity is the spark. Polarity is the passion. Polarity is the magnetism.

Daily Assessment

1. What does polarity mean to you?

____

____

____

____

2. Did you discover anything new about your own polarity? What was it?

____

____

____

____

3. Do you see how polarity affected your past relationships?

____

____

____

____

4. Have you been in competition with men? How?

5. How does it feel to evaluate your past relationships with this new information?

6. Did you discover the importance of polarity and how to make it work for you? How so?

Additional Notes:

DAY

2

Trust Your Heart

"When your heart speaks, take good notes." -Judith Campbell

Your heart is your inner guide. Your intuition. Your heart is connected to God (or whatever you choose to call the Divine). The heart gives its guidance when the mind is still and in solitude.

When you get out of your head you are able to get guidance from your heart. The reason is because the mind is always seeking answers but it isn't always open to the information that come from your inner guide.

The language of the mind is words, both written and spoken. And for the logical world this is great. But the heart doesn't speak in words --- it speaks in feelings, sensations, nudging and intuition.

The mind is masculine. The heart is feminine. The mind is based on logic, reasoning and the five senses. The heart is based on emotion and a sense of knowing and feeling.

When you learn to tune into your heart, you will find that you will know what to do in any given situation.

Once you learn to connect with your heart, you will discover the core of your femininity. The feminine is all about the heart. As the feminine counterpart, you are the heart of a relationship. You will start to cherish your feelings for they will provide the temperature of the relationship.

When you know how to connect with your heart, you will be able to silence the mind. When you question a situation where you feel like your heart and mind are in conflict, your heart wants priority but it will not demand attention from you. It is not pushy. But if you get in a quiet space you will get discernment from your heart about any doubts or questions you may have. This is why stillness is so important to recharging as a feminine woman.

Once you learn to listen and connect to your heart you will see all your fears, anxiety, and stress melt away. When you embrace your heart, you embrace your femininity. Femininity is an expression of your heart. You are able to let go of resistance and a need to control and just trust that as long as you are following your intuition everything will fall into place. This is not a tactic to change your men so that you can trust them, this is about you learning to trust yourself.

Today we are going to do a meditation that will get you out of your head and into your heart.

The Heart Centered Meditation

I want you to make sure that you are alone and are in comfortable clothing. It is very important that you will not be disturbed during this meditation.

Lay down on your bed or couch. Put your arms down by your side and straighten and relax your legs. Take a few deep breaths to the count of 5.

Continue to take deep breaths, in and out. Do this until you feel relaxed and as if you are becoming one with your bed.

Right now, if your mind is racing or is full of thoughts, just ignore them and let them go. Focus back on how relaxed you are.

You are beginning to relax. Now, begin to imagine that you are literally on a cloud in the sky. You can feel the softness as it melts into your body.

Breathing deeply.

Turn your focus on your heart. What do you feel? Are there any sensations? Do you feel a hunch?

Make sure you are tuned into your heart and not your mind. After you have identified what is going on with your heart bring yourself to awareness.

Now take some time to write about what you felt in the moment.

Do this exercise often so that you can get comfortable with the language of your heart.

Daily Assessment

1. What did you feel about the meditation?

____

____

____

____

2. Write down the details you experienced during this meditation?

____

____

____

____

3. Do you believe that you can trust your intuition to guide you? Why or why not?

____

____

____

____

4. How can listening to your heart help you make the right decisions with men?

____

____

____

____

Additional Notes:

DAY

3

FEMININE MYSTIQUE

"A woman is a warrior too. But she is meant to be a warrior in a uniquely feminine way." -Stasi Eldredge

I know you are wondering what in the world is feminine mystique? Well, first let me begin by telling you what it is not. It is not being coy, seductive, flirtatious, dramatic, or manipulative. Feminine mystique is about being your most authentic, vibrant, and passionate self by just being. You are just enjoying each moment and staying grounded in your heart.

A feminine woman is naturally mysterious to a man. She is the complete opposite of him, which intrigues and fascinates him. Her femininity draws him in because he cannot relate to the world the same way she does. She is feminine. He is masculine. It sparks his curiosity. Masculine and feminine see the world through different lenses. As we've learned, the polarity creates intense attraction.

A feminine woman is an enigma even if she isn't trying to be. A feminine woman is authentic and vulnerable. When you are authentic and vulnerable you are naturally mysterious because you are confident, high-value, rare and naturally magnetic. Most women today are quite the opposite due to feminist ideals and not understanding men. So, men are intrigued when they come across a woman who has feminine mystique.

Masculine men crave femininity because it compliments them. He needs femininity in order to be his best self. This is why women who are truly feminine have men flocking towards them. The appeal of femininity is that it is puzzling and he wants to experience more of it and "figure" it out. Men like to solve and "figure" things out. It's what being a man is to them.

A woman's mystery energizes and inspires a man to be in his most authentic, masculine self. It drives his natural protection and provider instincts. Her mystery sparks the polarity. This deepens the emotional connection for him. This is where he will feel respected and understood and you will feel cherished and adored. Men do not normally leave women of mystique. They are boomerangs, always bringing him back.

Contrary to what modern feminists have tried to promote, femininity is not about being a doormat, insecure or weak. It is a quieter strength. She is powerful even though she displays softness, playfulness, youthfulness, and emotional intelligence. She is secure in herself, yet so graceful. It is hard not to be affected by her humble power.

Masculine women and women who seek to be equal with men are the real weak women. They are trying to hide their insecurities by taking on energy that does not belong to them. They are not authentic and there is nothing weaker than living a false identity.

A mysterious woman operates from love and freedom, not fear and attachment. She makes a man feel like a hero. She makes a man feel needed without needing him. The problem with needing a man is that you are making him responsible for your fulfillment and happiness. That is not his job, that is an inside job. She accepts a man for his masculine strength and individuality and does not try to change him.

Being a mystery throughout your relationship is the key to his sustained connection and commitment. You should always keep a man guessing about you. He should never feel like he knows you completely. If you do this, you will find that a man will always be enamored by you. A man will continue to pursue you long after he has won you

Feminine mystique is the key to keeping him enchanted by you.

Feminine mystique is the characteristic that will have him thinking about you all day long. It keeps him curious about you. In your feminine mystique, you can keep a man curious about you for a lifetime. The only way to keep a man committed to you is to keep him wanting more: wanting to know you on a more profound level, wanting to feel what he feels when he hears your voice, wanting to feel more of what he feels when he is in your presence, wanting to know what the future with you holds, and wanting to be YOUR one and only. You will have a very deep effect on him. He will not want to be with other women, you are it for him. Every man wants a woman who makes him feel like he has arrived in his quest for "the one."

Ok, makes sense, how do I show feminine mystique?

Great, question. I will recap.

You achieve feminine mystique by being authentic. A masculine man finds a truly feminine woman mysterious just because she is feminine. A masculine man can understand and recognize (even subconsciously) masculinity but he cannot understand femininity. It baffles him in a good way that draws him in. Feminine women are meant to be mysterious to men in order to create that powerful polarity that we talk about so much.

So, embrace feminine mystique in order to keep a man devoted to you.

Daily Assessment

1. What are the perks of feminine mystique?

2. What are some ways that you can cultivate feminine mystique?

3. Have you ever associated femininity with weakness? Why?

4. How can you practice feminine mystique today?

Additional Notes:

DAY

4

F YOUR PAST

"To err is human; to forgive, divine." -Alexander Pope

So many women are living their lives today in bitterness, resentment, anger and unforgiveness; all hidden behind the illusion of self-contentment and independence. For some reasons, especially bordering on past unsavory experiences with men, they decide to go on rampage; waging an imaginary war against the opposite gender and of course, it is not rocket science to fathom why attracting and keeping quality men in their lives becomes such a huge problem. Being a feminine woman is more than just exhibiting certain behaviors, it is also about being open to love. You cannot be open to love if you are harboring negative emotions such as unforgiveness and bitterness. If you want to see some major shifts in your love life, you need to take heed of or pay heed to today's challenge. I want you to know that letting go of the past is paramount to becoming a feminine woman with hyper attractive qualities that will endear masculine men to you.

I know that today's challenge will be a major breakthrough for many of you. It was for me. I have personally seen women I've coached finally let go of the pain and hurt of the past and finally attract the type of men they've always wanted. You can do this too, if you are finally ready to forgive and move on—and ultimately enjoy the benefits.

Today is the day that you completely release your past and get unstuck from the rut you've found yourself. I want you to get ready to forgive everyone you feel has slighted you in the past or present.

You need to release your negative emotions so that you can stop attracting the same type of negative experiences in your love life. After you really let go, you will start to feel much lighter. Your heart will feel more open. When your heart is open, then you are ready for love. You are ready to attract the ideal man for you. And trust me, he will run to you.

Say it with Me: "I forgive all my past hurts, I open up the flow for my blessing to pour in. I open up the flow for true love to come to me."

Repeat this throughout the day until you feel it is your new life affirmation.

No matter what has happened to you. Let it go! Lay it down! Do not pick it back up! Do not look back at it!

After you do this exercise, you will wonder why you didn't forgive and let go a long time ago. You will feel like a mountain has been lifted off your shoulders. From this moment onward, I would advise you to practice forgiveness on a regular basis. Staying in a state of constant forgiveness will allow you to stay open to the flow of connection and love. Flow is a state of non-resistance. When you are in constant forgiveness you are in "flow" and when you are in flow, you are able to connect with your authentic feminine self. Femininity is about staying in flow and in vulnerability. We will talk more about vulnerability later.

For today's exercise, you will list all those who have caused you any pain in the past. You do not have to limit it to men, you can list friends, family and acquaintances. The guy who cut you off in traffic yesterday. FORGIVE! FORGIVE everyone you can think of who may have offended you in anyway.

Here is an example of what your list should look like:

- I forgive you, Martin for cheating on me. It hurt me but it helped me realize I was not a completely great wife myself. I was selfish and ignored your needs. Thank you, Martin, for what this experience has taught me. I release you in love.
- I forgive you, Julius, for ghosting me after 5 dates and never explaining why. I understand it might not have been easy to let me down. Thank you that this experience taught me discernment. I release you in love.
- I forgive you, Shantell, for sleeping with my boyfriend. It really hurt me, but it helped to stop being so naive in my friendships. Thank you for that lesson. I release you in love.

As you can see, the formula is to address the person by name, state what the offense was, what you learned from it, thank them for the lesson, and to release them in love. This technique will completely free you from the events that took place and give you absolute freedom to move forward to find the love of your life. Love and forgiveness are close friends and cannot stand to be apart. In fact, they will not tolerate separation.

I want you to come up with 25 situations to forgive. It may seem difficult at first but as you dig deep you will see the past hurts start to flow. Now you can clear them. The first time I did this exercise it really brought me to tears but afterwards my soul felt like a fresh rain had come through.

It felt so good, I've done it a few times just to make sure I have truly let go of certain events. So, without further ado let's get started on this thing, so that you can F the past!

Focused Forgiveness Exercise

You're about to forgive the hell out of some people, yay, let's go:

1. ______________________________
   ____
   ____
   ____
2. ______________________________
   ____
   ____
   ____
3. ______________________________
   ____
   ____
   ____
4. ______________________________
   ____
   ____
   ____
5. ______________________________
   ____
   ____
   ____
6. ______________________________
   ____
   ____

7.

8.

9.

10.

11.

12.

13.

14.

15.

16. ______________________________

17. ______________________________

18. ______________________________

19. ______________________________

20. ______________________________

21. ______________________________

22. ______________________________

23. ______________________________

24. ____
____
____
____

25. ____
____
____
____

After completing this exercise, how do you feel? You just released a lot of emotion, so you might have a mixture of feelings. It is ok. You have been emotionally backed up for years and you are detoxing. Just accept whatever comes up and know that everything will get better from this day onward. Be patient. This exercise, will transform all your relationships, not just the romantic ones. Do this exercise a couple more times, if you feel you still harbor some resentment or negativity. Most of all, I want you to remember to forgive yourself. You are doing the best you can. I am proud of you, you deserve relief.

Daily Assessment

1. How do you feel now?

____

____

____

____

2. Is there someone on the list that was hard to forgive? Why? Do you think you need to do this a few more times to really forgive?

____

____

____

____

3. Is there anyone you feel inclined to make things right with in person? Do so, if you feel a nudge, but this is not required for forgiveness to work. Trust your gut, your intuition.

____

____

____

____

Additional Notes:

DAY

5

Now Lean Back

"You don't need to justify your love, you don't need to explain your love, you just need to practice your love." -Miguel Ruiz

Leaning back means you detach from the outcome. You do not have an agenda. Leaning back is about mirroring his interests. You mirror his investment. You drop all expectations. You remove attachment. You are not concerned about where things are heading. You are not trying to control him or any situation. You just surrender to what is.

Examples of Leaning Forward

1. You have not heard from him, so you text him.
2. Your job just gave you free tickets to a Drake concert, so you decide to invite him.
3. You go onto his social media like all his pictures, statuses, comment, and watch every single one of his Snaps as soon as he posts them, hoping that he will remember you are alive.
4. After a date, you ask him when you will see him again.

5. He casually mentions getting together on Saturday afternoon. It is Saturday morning and you haven't heard from him so you text him to see if you guys are still on.
6. You ask him why he hasn't contacted you.
7. He has not introduced you to anyone but you introduce him to your mom.
8. You surprise him with dinner or a gift.
9. You go to his house and turn into Molly the Maid and Gordon Ramsey.
10. You "run" into him at the sports bar he goes to every Sunday.

The examples above show what is looks like to lean forward with a man. These scenarios are operating in masculine energy and show a woman who has an agenda. She is trying to control the outcome. Control feels like desperation to men. It is a major turn off and he will pull away.

When a woman is operating in masculine energy, a man feels uncomfortable and unsafe. On the flip side, feminine energy causes him to feel warm and comfortable.

Below are examples of leaning back to the same above scenarios.

Examples of Leaning Back

1. You don't ever initiate contact.
2. Your job just gave you free tickets to a Drake concert, you call and invite your best friend.
3. You haven't even added him back on your social media.
4. After a date, you thank him warmly and go about your business.
5. You didn't hear from him by Thursday so you already accepted a date with another man on your roster.
6. He hasn't contacted you? Tuh, you didn't notice. His number isn't even saved in your phone.
7. As far as he knows you have no friends or family.
8. You give yourself gifts.
9. You sit back, act as a guest, and let him attend to you at his house.
10. You stay the hell away from wherever he might be.

When you lean back you detach from the outcome and allow him to pursue you. He doesn't follow through, you knock him down on your roster and you keep it moving. No questions. No drama. Instead you stay leaned back in your feminine energy and thus stay attractive and magnetic.

Daily Assessment

4. In what ways have you been leaning forward?

5. Write 3 scenarios that are leaning forward and give opposite examples of leaning back.

6. Why do you feel the need to lean forward? What do you feel it accomplishes?

Additional Notes:

DAY

6

STOP DOING THE MOST

"Letting go doesn't mean that you don't care about someone anymore. It's just realizing that the only person you really have control over is yourself." -Deborah Reber

Yesterday, you saw how unattractive leaning forward is and why you need to practice leaning back. You need to learn the very effective art of being. Not doing, just being. Not giving, but receiving. Not thinking, but feeling. You just need to commit to stop doing anything that feels like "work" around a man.

If you want to be the feminine energy counterpart in the relationship, then you need to stop operating in masculine energy. You are taking away the pleasure of being a man from your man. A man gets his worth in being actively involved in; doing, thinking, and managing counterpart in the relationship. This is what it means to be masculine.

By doing so much you are telling him that you do not trust him to provide, take care of you, and cherish your femininity. When you do everything in a relationship you are telling a man that he is unable to make you happy.

What happens when you do too much?

He will begin to become lazy and complacent in your relationship. He will slowly stop making any effort to make you happy. He will just sit back and let you do all the work until it gets to be too much for him. A man needs to express his masculinity so if he cannot do it with you he will find another way. He will go to where his masculinity is welcomed. He may start cheating and/or eventually leave.

You are used to taking actions in your interactions with men because it makes you feel like you are in control. You thought if you can control the direction and the outcome of the relationship you will be able to get everything you want out of a man. But this control is false. Love cannot be controlled. It is limitless and expansive and should be allowed to roam freely. When you let go of the need to take control and just enjoy each moment and check in with how you feel, you open up the door for true intimacy to come in. You are able to be vulnerable. Vulnerability goes a long way with establishing a connection with a man.

I believe most women do too much in a relationship because they want to be appreciated. However, it never works because appreciation is what the masculine energy wants. As long as you are dealing with a masculine man you will never get appreciation for what you 'do.'

The feminine energy gets appreciation for just being who she is, not from doing.

So, stop! Stop doing the most!

Today, I want you to stop doing the most in your relations with men. You will stop doing everything that has not served you in the past. You will stop trying to earn your way into a man's heart. You will commit to putting yourself first and your feelings. You will not pretend or play hard to get. You will authentically own your femininity.

Decide today that you will stop relying on action to connect with a man. Decide today that you will stop trying to control men and relationships. Decide today that you will instead relax and embrace your feminine nature. The more you make these decisions the easier it is to change your mindset and start embracing a new way to attract the high-quality masculine men that you want that are open to love.

Today's action is simple. You will practice putting yourself first and connecting with your feelings. Let go of what anyone else might think of you or what other obligations you might have today. Today is all about you.

Daily Assessment

Today you will do one activity to put yourself first. This activity is all about you. It could be going on a walk, getting a massage, going to the gym, getting an ice cream, going to your favorite restaurant, or buying those shoes that were on sale. The list is endless. After you have done this activity, come back here and answer the following questions.

1. What activity did you choose? Why?

____

____

____

____

2. How did it feel to put yourself first?

____

____

____

____

3. What were 3 emotions you felt today?

4. Did you feel guilt or uncomfortable while going about your activity? If so, why?

5. What are some ways you do too much with men?

In case you felt any type of guilt or a similar emotion, you deserved the time you took for yourself, today. I am proud of you!

Additional Notes:

DAY

7

Masculine Respect

"In modern society, there are fewer and fewer opportunities for men to be men. For masculinity to flourish in all its glory." -Milo Yiannopoulos

To a man respect is love. A man cannot feel loved if he is not respected. Respect is the highest need for a man. A man who does not feel he is respected by his woman will not commit to her because he does not trust her. Trust and respect go hand in hand with men. A man who does not feel respected cannot feel trust.

Respecting a man is about understanding that his ego is tied to how he feels about himself when he is around you. Respecting his masculinity will set his attraction for you on fire. Masculine respect fulfills the subconscious prerequisite he needs before he feels it's safe to let his guard down. When he lets his guard down he has given you direct access to penetrate his heart.

I have coached a few clients on how to respect their men and the changes in their relationship have improved drastically.

The best way to make sure that you are respecting the masculine is by following these 5 rules:

The 5 Rules of Masculine Respect

1. **Give up trying to control him.**

I have spoken about control before but now I will tell you why it is important to your partner. Trying to control a man, makes him feel incompetent, useless and like a small child. Examples:

" You need to call me more."

"I need you to do this...that."

"Take the kids to school."

Seeing a man and approaching him first.

Inviting him anywhere.

Initiating any type of contact.

2. **Give up trying to control the outcome/situation.**

This right here is probably one of the fastest ways to kill attraction with a man. Trying to move the relationship or lack thereof forward is the best example of this. Trying to move things forward looks like offering to pay for anything, planning dates/outings, trying to get something out of him, pretty much DOING anything. As I stated before, doing is masculine. Relax.

3. **Give up the 7 Deadly C's.**

Trying to manage a man or a relationship is very disrespectful to the role of the masculine energy and looks like:

coercing - "If you don't do this, then there will be no sex."

criticizing - "You are not doing this right. Let me do it."

condemning - "I hate when you do that."

counseling - "You really should do things in this manner."

cautioning - "If I were you, I would think twice before…."

coaxing - "Oh, please, pretty, pretty please…"

calculating - "Zale's is having a huge sale on diamonds..."

4. **Give up trying to change him.**

If you cannot accept a man for who he is right now, not who he has the potential to be, but who he is right now, please leave him alone. There is nothing that will make a man flee away from you faster than trying to change him in anyway. If you do not like a man for who he is, he is not the one for you and you are not the one for him.

5. **Give up your need for a 'yes.'**

If a man says "no" about going to that concert with you, you accept it. You do not try to guilt trip him, ask for reasons and explanations, use manipulations or any of those things. You let it go. You go by yourself or with someone else.

As you can see, these 5 rules will pretty much stop all conflict in your interactions with men. When you stop doing these things, you will show your man you respect his masculinity and leadership. Later we will talk about what to do to communicate since you have stopped most of how you communicate with him. There will probably be lot of silence now. That is good. It is better to be silent than to risk emasculating your man and losing his attraction for you. For now, let's get ready to dive into today's assessment.

Daily Assessment

1. In what ways, if any, have you been disrespecting the masculine?

____

____

____

____

2. Which of the 7 Deadly C's do you commit the most?

____

____

____

____

3. What is your key takeaway from today's lesson?

____

____

____

____

Additional Notes:

DAY

8

Receive, Reciprocate, Repeat

'Women still dream and hope, pin their emotions on some man who doesn't reciprocate, and end up in confusion. -Elizabeth Elliott

Masculine men fall in love while giving to you. They fall in love when you are receptive to their giving. And lastly, they fall in love with how you are able to reciprocate their efforts.

Biologically, women are meant to receive. During intercourse, you receive a man into you and at the time of orgasm you receive his ejaculation. So, based on nature, the way to intimacy with a man is when you are open and receptive to his giving. When you are comfortable sitting back and receiving you are in your true feminine nature.

How can I receive?

When a man offers or does anything for you to show his affection or to help you in one way or the other, you accept it warmly. If he offers to fix something at your house, you let him and you say, 'thank you,' excitedly. You do not say, "No, I got it. I can do it!" When you reject a man's giving, you reject his masculinity and you have missed an opportunity to build attraction and connection between you.

You need to get comfortable receiving and reciprocating in order to show your appreciation. A masculine man wants to give to the woman of his affections and he wants her to appreciate his efforts. He wants to be the man and step up and show out, but he can only do what you let him do.

Men are simple. They gravitate toward women who make them feel good. A man feels good when he is able to be in his masculine energy (giving) and you are in your feminine energy (receiving). It is a beautiful well-choreographed dance.

Then you reciprocate his giving to show your appreciation. Behind respect, appreciation is the second highest need of a man.

How do you reciprocate?

Well let's say a man has been consistent in his efforts and have taken you on 5 nice dates (he picked you up, he paid, told you goodnight, etc.).

For the 6th date, you can offer to cook him dinner at your place. This way you are reciprocating his efforts and showing him appreciation for his consistency in pursuing you. This is also effective because it shows him that you are not just a person who takes and takes and is selfish. You are also giving him a preview of your cooking skills (can you say 'wife material?'). But you are not taking the lead which allows him to do so and he feels comfortable to continue to pursue you.

So, in order to capture the heart of the masculine man in your life you have to stop giving first, which is a form of control, and start receiving and reciprocating with appreciation to what he is giving to you. He should be coming toward you, pursuing you while you are laid back and taking in all the attention with warmth and enthusiasm and every so often match his effort with a token of appreciation.

Some of the ways that you can reciprocate and show appreciation for the man in your life are:

- Buying him a small token.
- Keeping his favorite beer in your fridge
- Calling him handsome, after he called you beautiful
- Giving him your undivided attention when you are on the phone or in his presence.

- Answering the phone warmly.

Being a more feminine woman takes strength, especially for the modern woman who is used to being masculine. It takes a strong woman to sit back and relinquish control. It takes a strong woman to receive happily without guilt. It takes a strong woman to know how to reciprocate. It takes an even stronger woman to understand how this dynamic is essential to getting men to cherish her.

Daily Assessment

1. Do you feel like you are the one always giving in your relationship? How has that worked for you? How has that made you feel?

____

____

____

____

2. Do you feel that you have to show a man that you are interested or he will lose interest? How has that worked for you?

____

____

____

____

3. Do you find that you feel slighted in love often? Do you wonder why you give so much to men and they just disappear, ghost and stop making any effort?

____

____

4. Do you find that you become needy and clingy in your interactions because men keep pulling away?

5. List 3 instances you can reciprocate with a man.

Additional Notes:

DAY

9

FEMININITY IS THE JUICE

"They asked her, "how did you free yourself?" She answered, "by embracing my own power." -Yung Pueblo

A woman's femininity is her power. If a man can "figure" out what a woman is about she isn't living in her authentic nature and her attractive pull is weak. A woman isn't supposed to make sense to a man, she is supposed to make him feel curiosity, intrigue, and merriment. The sensuality and sexuality of a woman draws men in from afar. It's like moths to a flame.

Feminine energy is about feeling, expressing, intuiting, just being, following, creating and receiving. Your feminine energy is about how you engage with a man to ignite this masculine energy. To be in your feminine energy means you are comfortable with listening to your intuition and expressing your feelings. You live in the moment with a zest for life.

The main thing that makes the feminine woman so attractive to a masculine man is that she is able to make him FEEL. The masculine man is always thinking, planning and just in his head so much that he usually is not capable of accessing his feelings. However, when he is in the presence of a feminine woman who expresses her feelings, he is able to access HIS feelings. This is why masculine seeks feminine, to access his heart.

When you are open to your feminine energy with him, you give him a safe place to express his masculine energy to you. And when the exchanges of energy are flowing back and forth between each other - a true heart connection is made. A man falls in love with a woman who gets him out of his head and into his heart. He falls in love with a woman for reasons he cannot name, not because she is sexy, sweet or successful. When asked he will say, "It's just something about her." That "something" is her ability to touch his heart by her first touching her own heart.

If you like the idea of being with a masculine man (a man who leads, initiates, actualizes, etc.) then it is important that you become a feminine woman.

Embodying your feminine energy will get you all the affection and adoration in a relationship you want. You embody your feminine energy by tuning into how you feel, trusting those feelings and expressing those feelings. It means being committed to what is right for you based on those feelings. It means practicing and being comfortable with vulnerability.

You dance. You cry. You laugh. You play. You are relaxed and going with the flow as long as it feels good to you.

The feminine is about connection. When you can own your feminine essence, you can connect with anyone. You can form all relationships easily, including lasting friendships. When a woman is connected she is thriving. She is connected to life and love. And life and love come back to her full throttle. She does not need to earn the love or approval of anyone.

Her being magnetizes men to her like a single focused laser. They want to get more of what she offers because it is overflowing onto them. She has all the juiciness men can't explain but crave.

Daily Assessment

1. Based on what you learned today, what is femininity to you?

____

____

____

____

2. Are you committed to embracing your feminine essence so that you can attract the type of man you want? How?

____

____

____

____

3. Let's practice tuning into your feelings, trusting them, and expressing them. What do you feel about your love life right now? Why do you feel that? Do you feel comfortable expressing how you feel?

____

____

____

____

Additional Notes:

DAY 10

He's Already Been Raised

"You can't raise a man, he's already grown, what you gonna do?" -K. Michelle

I have talked about control so many times before, and how it will have a man fleeing from you in a nanosecond, but today, I want to talk about a specific form of control: mothering. Mothering is the worse and most common way women emasculate men. Men lose all attraction for women who act like their mother. A man doesn't want to fuck his mom. The idea repulses him and so will any woman who acts like his mother.

What is mothering?

Mothering is when you are doing things for him he didn't ask you to do, giving him an opinion or advice, he didn't ask you for. You tell him what to do and how to live his life. You think you are being helpful or nurturing but you are not. You are, however, emasculating him. Neither does a man need a woman to tell him how TO DO anything nor does he want her to tell him WHAT TO DO. Keep all unsolicited advice, comments, and criticisms to yourself. The best rule to remember is when in doubt, keep quiet.

Mothering is a huge turn off to men. It does nothing but pushes him away. Some may call it nurturing. Some may call it being a ride or die. Some may say it's being a good woman. Whatever you call it, it's a turnoff to men. It kills all the attraction in him. Men want a woman who they can take home to their mom, not be their mom.

Mothering a man tells him you do not trust him to be a man. You are telling him you know how to be a man more than he does. You are telling him that he cannot figure out his life without your help and guidance. He will begin to feel unsafe, hindered and that he cannot be himself. He will go seek out a woman who allows him to feel safe being him and being the leader in the relationship he was born to be.

A common theme I see in relationships are women seeing potential in a man and taking him on as a project to get him to this potential they believe he has. This is a huge mistake, you are taking away who he is as a man. If you cannot accept a man for who he is today then you are the wrong woman for him and you need to release him. Do not try to better him. He will grow to resent you as his attraction for you goes down to zero.

So, if you feel that you need to direct, control, or advise a man then you are mothering him. This is never good. A man is not looking for a replacement mom. He is looking for a partner who knows how to support him from her feminine essence. When you do this, he will be inspired to step up himself and be the man you need, if he is the right man for you.

Daily Assessment

1. In what ways have you mothered a man?

____

____

____

____

2. Where did your mothering behavior originate?

____

____

____

____

3. What is the opposite of mothering?

____

____

____

____

4. What can you do today to stop mothering your man? Or a future man?

____

5. Explain why mothering is a huge turn off to men?

Additional Notes:

DAY 11

YOUR EGO WILL KEEP YOU SINGLE

"Nobody sees anybody truly but all through the flaws of their own egos. That is the way we all see each other in life. Vanity, fear, desire, competition-- all such distortions within our own egos-- condition our vision of those in relation to us." -Tennessee Williams

The ego is not your amigo. If you are a member of my Facebook group, Feminine Magnetism—Your Superpower, you would have heard me talk about the ego extensively and how it does not serve your interest. The ego will keep you single because it will keep you defensive and in constant upset. The ego does not want us to become vulnerable. The ego does not belong in a relationship because the ego cannot fit into the construct of a relationship. A relationship is about connection; however, the ego is about conflict, drama, and separation.

If you want to have a successful love life, you must learn to tame your ego. Throughout my journey, in my own love life, I have realized the importance of being a humble person who is not controlled by my ego.

Because of my psychology background, I have put some research into the ego and how to overcome it. No doubt, I'm still a work in progress but I am able to discern when my ego is rearing its ugly head and choose an alternative response. The ego is very manipulative and controlling. It's impossible to completely overcome the ego but as long as you mostly control it and it doesn't mostly control you, then cheers, you have arrived.

The ego is the enemy of femininity because it is based in fear. Fear is the inverse of vulnerability. Vulnerability is the core of femininity. In order to connect with a masculine man, as I have said before; you must tune into your femininity and your vulnerability. The ego is all about itself it does not care about connection, it does not care about love, it does not care about couple hood it only cares about being right and self-validation albeit at another person's expense.

This is why so many women are not able to make a connection with a man because they are so ego-driven. The ego makes things hard for us because it does not want to fall in line, rather it wants to exert its dominance and it wants to be the most important aspect of any interactions we have with others. The ego is very reliant on self-importance. Love is not hard at all, connection is not hard at all, relationship is not hard at all, joy is not hard at all. The conflicting ego is what makes things hard for us.

What is the ego?

The ego is the part of yourself that thrives on separation and conflict. It is the part of yourself that is comprised of your beliefs and perspectives. It creates and aims to protect your self-identity. This identity the ego has constructed is around self-importance and self-preservation and it does anything to stay comfortable in this identity it has created.

When it's presented with information that it recognizes as true but challenges the identity it has created, it causes you to feel attacked and offended. In this way, you are too busy defending your identity to heed the changes or truth in the new information. You stay stuck in the same patterns and the ego is happy.

Possessiveness, neediness, attachment, and fear all come from the ego. These traits are very, very detrimental to a relationship. What rises up is the need for power and control based off of these negative traits. The second we feel like a partner or potential partner is pulling away from us or rejecting us our ego raises its hideous head. The ego causes us to close the gap and act. It causes us to start pursuing our men in order to "fix" things and to ease what we sense is rejection. The ego cannot handle rejection, whenever the ego feels rejected it acts like a little child having a temper tantrum and if you are not self-aware it can cause you to lash out at others.

The ego also loves to play the blame game. It is always 'his' fault. You are an innocent victim who never does anything wrong. The whole world is out to get you especially this man or that man. When you start dating, all of the fears and insecurities that you had before come to the surface. So, you can either blame others or you can deal with your shit. Deal with your shit so that you can attract better or improve existing relationships.

Relationships challenge us. They cause us to grow. They bring up all of the nasty stuff that we really don't want to deal with. But love will bring up all those things that are not lovely so that you can release them. And remember that the issues that you keep having in every relationship are the ones that you really need to focus on. But your ego wants you to believe that you keep having these issues because other people are the problem and you are perfect. Don't blame him or the outside world. Instead, take responsibility for creating your own circumstances and make love and connection your priority; not useless drama and ego struggles.

Taming the ego is important because it will keep you out of your feminine essence. The ego does not like vulnerability because it means it has to acknowledge its wounding and remember the ego thinks it's already perfect and does not need to change.

If you want to establish a deep connection with a man, you must release your ego. You must be open to criticism from those who know more than you and you must be open to your man. Be open by choosing connection over being right.

Daily Assessment

Today I want to give you affirmations that will help to reprogram your mind and to get out of your ego and into connection.

"I am open to love. I am open to trust. I am open to connection. I let go of fear. I let go of worry. I let go of blame. I let go of everything that does not serve me on my journey to finding the perfect partner for me. I am surrounded by people who love me. I love my life. I love myself. I love those around me. Because I am surrounded by love I accept my flaws. I accept correction. I accept constructive criticism. I feel liberated from my worries. I feel liberated from my fears. I feel liberated from negative ego responses. I am gentle with myself knowing that I am doing the best that I can and I open my heart. My heart is open and receptive. My heart remains open no matter what the situation is. My light does not dim. I open myself up to vulnerability because I deserve authentic connection and genuine love. I love myself."

Now answer the following:

1. How did you feel before you did the affirmations?

   ____

   ____

   ____

2. How did you feel while you were saying the affirmations?

3. What thoughts came up as you were reciting the affirmations?

4. Any issues that you have repressed come up?

5. How did you feel after you finished the affirmations?

Additional Notes:

DAY 12

NO DOORMAT ZONE

"If they aren't treating you right, it's time to stop blaming them. You decide your worth, so if you don't want to be a doormat, get off the floor." -Charles Orlando

When many think of 'being feminine' they think of being a doormat. It is thought that femininity is synonymous to being weak minded. Femininity, however, is the opposite of weakness. A truly feminine woman is a powerhouse.

You should never let a man (or anyone for that matter) walk over you. There is nothing more unattractive to a man than a woman who doesn't have any boundaries and standards and lets him walk all over her like she's a plush rug.

Being a doormat means that you do whatever he wants you to do or what you think would please him without first tuning into yourself to see if that is what you want to do or how you feel about it. You constantly ignore red flags and make excuses. You feel guilty, feel undeserving, and feel "bad" when he mistreats you. You tell yourself the false narrative that if you just do what he wants he will love, cherish and commit to you, someday.

This approach will never work for you. A man will never respect a woman who does not respect herself. He will never respect a woman who puts him before herself at her own peril and happiness. He will just use you up, throw you away and find and commit to a woman with standards and self-respect.

Stop. Stop putting men who are not your husband before you. Get in tune with your feelings and what you want and start going in that direction. It may be scary initially to put yourself first and to believe and have courage that you are capable of getting love by standing up for yourself. But you have to remember if you do not stand up for yourself, who will? If you do not love yourself, who will? Let me tell you who, no one!

A man cannot connect with a woman who is not being authentic. A doormat is not being authentic, you are ignoring your true self. You are craving that the man in your life will give you what you refuse to give yourself. He will not. It all starts with you. Give yourself what you want to receive.

Take responsibility for your life. Being a doormat means that you have handed over the reins of your life to someone else and you are just crossing your fingers hoping everything works out in your favor. This is not the way to get his commitment.

The solution is to instead tune into your feminine energy. The key is to put your heart first. Look into your emotions and own them and speak from them. Speak from your emotions to communicate boundaries. When something feels good, say it. When something does not feel good, say it. When you want to do something, say it. When you don't want to do something, say so. This is how a man can trust you. He can trust you because you are being true to yourself. We trust those who are truthful.

You have to let go of the fear that if you exert your standards and boundaries that he will be turned off or go away. He will not. He will feel safer with you because he can trust that you will keep it real with him. But if for some reason he does leave, then you dodged a bullet. The right man will never leave you for being true to yourself and your boundaries. Men love standards. Remember to do what is in the best interest for your heart.

Daily Assessment

1. What did you think a doormat meant before today?

____

____

____

____

Are there times you have been a doormat? How did it feel?

____

____

____

____

2. Are you ready to put yourself first in dating? How committed are you?

____

____

____

____

Additional Notes:

DAY 13

HERE'S HOW TO GET HIM TO DO WHAT YOU WANT

"Our anxiety does not come from thinking about the future, but wanting to control it."
-Kahlil Gibran

Once you begin to let go of control, and allow your man to take the lead you will begin to see that he wants to do everything he possibly can to make you happy. Your man now feels confident in the fact that he can make you happy, he will look for ways to make you happy, and he will make it his mission to make you happy. When you stop telling a man what to do, that is when it will be easy to get him to do what you want him to do.

So how do you get him to do what you want him to do?

I have already explained to you what doesn't work when communicating with the masculine energy. So now, it is time to explain to you what does work when communicating with masculine men.

Today, you will learn how to express yourself in an authentic and feminine way that will inspire him to give you exactly what you want and need. Since you are no longer telling him what to do, he will not: withdraw, shut down, or become defensive. Instead he will become enchanted with you and he will want to know what is going on with you, what are you feeling and how he can become your hero.

This is the perk of expressing yourself femininely. Expressing yourself and your needs in this way will avoid drama and control. You will simply get in tune with your feelings and then you will express yourself without blame from those feelings. Doing this will get you in touch with his heart and he will feel inspired to give you what you want and what you need.

Major key alert: understanding this simple concept today will be the main ingredient that will get you the relationship that you have always dreamt of with a high-quality masculine man.

The first step is to identify h*ow* you feel.

Being feminine is about being in your feelings, but not in *your feelings* in the messy, dramatic, and petty way that does not work with men. Being in the feminine means you are in tune with your feelings and emotions and you are expressing yourself from that place. This is the opposite of control, you are simply expressing how you feel at any given moment and expressing what you want and what you don't want, what you will accept and what you will not accept, what feels good and what doesn't feel good in a way that will compel a man to step up. The masculine man cannot resist a woman who expresses herself to him in feminine energy. His natural instinct is to make the feminine happy. This is the power of the feminine.

I understand that this is a new concept for many, so today we will do an exercise to help you to tune into and recognize your feelings. You cannot express your feelings to a man if you are not able to identify those feelings and feel comfortable with those feelings. Do not be afraid of your feelings. You may have heard that men do not like feelings, but the truth is that they do not like drama. Drama is what happens when a woman is full of fear and tries to control situations. Drama is when you make a man responsible for your happiness. You place the blame on him instead of checking your expectations. This attack and blame on a man causes instant withdrawal and defensiveness in him as his masculinity is being challenged. It feels terrible to him and all he wants to do is get away. But now you know better and you will do better. So, let's get started.

"Feel the Feeling" Exercise

I want you to sit down in a comfortable chair or lay down on your back with your arms to your side, legs stretched out and together and close your eyes. Now focus on your breath. Breathe in to the count of four, hold it, now breathe out to the count of four. Do these seven times. Now you should be relaxed and very comfortable.

Now I want you to take a deep breath; feel the breath expand your body, now breathe out and as you breathe out pay attention to what is coming from your heart. Do not pay attention to your thoughts, pay attention to your heart—tune into the voice of your heart.

Now ask your heart for a feeling. Say, "Dear heart, what do you feel right now?" Listen intently to the answer. Do not judge the answer or be in denial of the answer. It will be an emotion or some type of sensation in your body. What came up? Anger? Fear? Sadness? Bliss? Excitement? Embarrassment? Disappointment? Remember these are your feelings and they do not have anything to do with anyone else. Examples of sensations are: 'I feel cold.' 'I feel hungry.' 'I feel butterflies in my stomach.'

Now, once you have located your feelings and/or sensations. Thank your heart for responding to you and now you can open your eyes. Immediately dive into today's assessment.

Daily Assessment

1. Did you locate a feeling or sensation?

____

____

____

____

2. What emotions and/or sensations came up?

____

____

____

____

3. Was it easy to come up with an emotion or sensation?

____

____

____

____

4. How do you feel overall about this exercise? Was it Scary? Relieving? Something else?

5. What is the difference between expressing your feelings and being dramatic?

Additional Notes:

DAY 14

YOU ARE WORTHY

"You are worthy of love and respect. You are beautiful, gifted, and intelligent. Don't let the storm make you forget that." -Thema Davis

I want you to realize that you are worthy of the love you desire. You are worthy of the love you desire!

I want you to become a goddess. I want you to know how to be a high value woman who knows her worth. That has this certain vibe that emanates effortlessly and magnetizes any man that comes across your path. It comes from unwavering self-love and self-esteem.

This has nothing to do with your outside beauty. You are attractive beyond the physical. You have personality, self-confidence and charisma that makes men addicted to you. You embrace your feminine charm and sexuality. You are not using your sexuality as a bargaining chip but a vehicle for bonding and self-expression.

You have got to understand that you are the key to attracting the man of your dreams. As a woman, you are the most important part of a relationship, you are the heartbeat of the relationship. You need to embrace your power and stop handing it over to men. You have got to put yourself first. You also must remain open to love. You cannot shut down because you have had some bad experiences.

When you recite things like, "I'm never going to find the one", "Men suck", "There are no good men left", "All men cheat", you are telling the universe to continue to give you the same crap you have been getting. Change your vibe, to change your tribe.

The more you torment yourself ruminating over the mistakes that you have made in the past with men, the further away you get from seeing your own self-worth. When you don't see your self-worth, you do not realize that all of those mistakes are preparing you to receive the man that is meant for you if you take the steps to truly become feminine and understand men.

Baby girl, in order to attract a high-quality man, you have to believe that you deserve a high-quality man. High quality men know that they are high quality, and they only want a woman who also thinks of herself as high-quality. You cannot attract a man of high worthwhile you are hanging in the lower worth corner.

There is a saying going around stating that you date at the level of your self-esteem, and nothing could be truer. In the past, you have attracted men who didn’t see your worth not because you didn’t have any worth, but because you didn't see your own worth so there was nothing there for them to see. If there is something missing in your love life it's because there's something that you aren't giving out. You can never receive what you do not give and the giving must start with yourself.

A feminine woman embraces herself for who she is now while working on becoming the best version of herself. Even though she accepts herself, and loves herself, and sees her worth she knows that there is always room for improvement. Just because you are working to improve yourself does not mean that you are not already worthwhile. Embrace the change, embrace the new perspective that this book and my other teachings give you about dating and love but never feel like you aren't already a priceless gem and an absolute goddess, because you are.

So, in order to get the type of relationship you want, you have to change the way you view yourself. Relationships are mirrors. What you see out there is a reflection of what is going on inside of you.

Change your beliefs about yourself, men, relationships, the feminine, the masculine, and what you deserve in a relationship. This is the foundation of how you will move past what is keeping you stuck in the same dead-end pattern. Once you are able to identify and clarify what it is you really want, you will realize your self-worth. This is how you will manifest your "happily ever after".

Daily Assessment

1. Have you struggled with low self-worth in the past?

____

____

____

____

2. How do you think having low self-worth has affected past relationships?

____

____

____

____

3. Are you willing to change your beliefs and perspectives in order to receive the relationship that you want?

____

____

____

____

4. What are the consequences of continuing not to value yourself?

5. What do you believe to be the source of your low self-worth?

6. What is the actual truth about yourself? What is the truth about your worth?

7. Using #6, write an affirmation stating your worth in the present tense. Recite this affirmation daily until you believe it to be a certified fact.

8. How do you feel after writing that affirmation?

Additional Notes:

DAY

15

VULNERABILITY IS THE SECRET SAUCE

"Vulnerability is the only authentic state. Being vulnerable means being open, for wounding, but also for pleasure. Being open to the wounds of life means also being open to the bounty and beauty. Don't mask or deny your vulnerability: it is your greatest asset."
-Stephen Russell

In order to make a heart connection with a man you must be vulnerable. Remember, you are the heartbeat of a relationship: you have got to open yourself up first. A man can never open his heart up to a woman who hasn't first made herself vulnerable to him. In order to form a connection with a man you must be authentic, open to love, and receptive.

Being vulnerable is the key to building a heart centered connection with a man.

Being vulnerable can be scary but it is also the most rewarding part of a relationship. You become vulnerable when you stop trying to control situations with men, when you stop trying to lead situations with men, when you stop over-thinking situations with men, and when you stop doing more than your fair share with men. Then you are able to step into your feminine essence: showing appreciation and expressing your feelings. Yes, this can be scary because you are no longer in a false sense of control, now you have to let go and trust the process. You do not need to trust a man, you need to trust your feelings and you need to trust the process. The process is putting yourself first, setting up standards, and only tolerating situations that feel good to you every moment.

I know in today's age, women have allowed the fuckboys of the world to harden their hearts. You are so terrified of being played that you run from intimacy, closeness and connection. But if you continue to run, you will find yourself tired and still alone.

Since, a lot of women have felt that men have failed them, they have decided to be their own man. They have put armor around their heart and sealed up their vulnerability.

You tell yourselves that you can do the same things that men do. You tell yourselves that you can play the game same way as men. You tell yourselves that you can have casual sex and not catch feelings. You tell yourselves that you are independent women who do not need men. You tell yourselves that you are educated and financially stable and do not need a man for anything other than sex. You tell yourselves that you can think like men and beat them at their own game. You tell yourselves that you are equal to men. But in actuality all you are doing is feeding yourself a whole bunch of bullshit that is keeping you single and empty. Everything you are telling yourself to keep you safe behind that stack of cards is a lie. Deep down you know that it is a lie but it protects you from your fear of exposure and your fear of being out of control. These lies, however, are doing nothing but keeping you lonely, bitter and full of regret.

Because you are afraid to be vulnerable - you subconsciously choose men who do not want you, men who are afraid of commitment, feminine men, fuckboys, and narcissists. Or even worse you never get back out there in the dating world, you fall and never get back up.

There is a better way. Instead of putting up a front, you need to set up boundaries and standards. This way you protect your heart by standing up for it in an authentic manner. If you follow your feelings you will find that you will not need to be afraid of being hurt. Your boundaries and standards will not allow you to accept anything that is not serving you. Standards and boundaries minimize hurt. Then you can feel comfortable surrendering your heart in order to connect with a man.

It is true that dating is scary. You do not know if you will have a future with this man or if he will play you. But vulnerability says, "Even though I am afraid because I have no control over what may happen between this man and myself, I surrender to the process by establishing my boundaries and standards, trusting my feelings, and honoring those feelings in every moment."

Boundaries are lines that you will not allow to be crossed. For example, you have established a boundary that a man cannot meet your children until you guys are engaged. Another example, is you do not allow men into your home on the first date. A standard is a personal constitution by which you live your life. A standard could be that you date for marriage, you do not date just to date. A standard is that you date men who are emotionally available.

So yes, love is risky and being vulnerable is even riskier but if you are not vulnerable you will never experience true love.

As I stated earlier, you must go first, terrified, trembling and surrendered. The feminine is responsible for the feelings of the relationship. Therefore, the masculine will not be able to open up to his feelings until the feminine exposes her feelings, lays them raw on the table, and puts down the walls that she has built. When you do this, the right man for you will honor your feelings and worship your vulnerability.

Vulnerability is the secret sauce.

Daily Assessment

1. What does it feel like to just let go? What does it feel like to surrender?

____

____

____

____

2. What would happen if I rewrite the protective narratives I've told myself to protect myself from being hurt?

____

____

____

____

3. What would happen if I let go of control and traded it for connection?

____

____

____

____

4. What are 3 boundaries/ standards I can establish right now that will be my guide book?

____

____

____

____

5. Am I willing to let go of the walls I have built around my heart? How?

____

____

____

____

6. In what ways in the past did I choose fear over intimacy and vulnerability?

____

____

____

____

7. Am I willing to let go of my trust issues surrounding men and instead trust myself?

Additional Notes:

DAY

16

BUILD A ROSTER

"You have as many options as you give yourself." -Kasie West

Now the fun begins! It's time to let go of the girlfriend mindset. Being a girlfriend (friends with benefits, baby mama, side chick or any other unmarried relations) is a trap. I want to emphasis the important of keeping a rotation of men for your sanity. Rotating men, will help you to remain in your power as you see that you truly are the prize.

What is a roster?

A roster is a group of men you are dating simultaneously with the purpose of marriage. The magic number is three. If you can handle more men then great, but three is a good start. Having a roster allows you to take control of your love life, you are not at the mercy of any man. When you date one man exclusively, also known as being a girlfriend, you are waiting for him to either dump you or marry you. Your waiting can go on for years possibly decades. The way to take back your power is to commit yourself to the relationship that you want not to any one man.

That commitment to a relationship begins with a roster. Building a roster isn't necessarily about finding the one, it is about learning how to interact with men, learning what you like and it is also about building your confidence. It's about learning your limits and practicing your standards so that you can be ready for the man of your dreams.

Building a roster protects you. It keeps you from investing too much emotionally into one man who may not be the one for you. It keeps you in control of your heart. Keeping a roster is all about putting your needs first. You are essentially putting up standards. A man will understand that in order to get what he desires from you, he has to fully commit to the type of relationship that you want.

Keeping a roster will ensure that you are in your feminine energy. When you have these men pursuing you, you are able to lean back and enjoy the ride. You have a certain confidence that is very attractive to men. You are attractive because you are allowing men to do what they are designed to do: pursue. Men love a woman who has a relaxed energy that allows him to chase her. Men are designed to be the one chasing, pursuing, and doing in a relationship or they will never build any attraction with a woman.

You have to understand that dating is all about numbers. The more options you have the better selection you have. Every man you meet will not be the one. If you make the mistake of becoming exclusive with a man who isn't the one you will have wasted days, weeks, months, and possibly years on one man. In that timeframe, you could have met another man who could have been your future husband.

Also, when you date one man and it doesn't work out you will have to start all over again with a broken heart. There is no broken heart in roster dating because you are not investing yourself into just one man, your focus is divided so that you will not make any one man too important. This prevents heartbreak and hurt feelings.

In this way, you respond to pursuit instead of pursuing. You are allowing yourself to be the prize that you are.

No matter what a man says, men love competition. Men pursue women who they deem are high-value and one of the ways men deem a woman high value is his perception of her having other male suitors. If a man believes that he is your only option he will not see you as that worthwhile. Things of value are wanted and pursued by many.

Today I will give you a challenge to go out there and begin building your roster. I want you to get comfortable with the idea of putting your needs first by diverting your attention to multiple men so that you will not get hung up on any one man.

For today's exercise, I want you to do two things: 1) I want you two have a pep talk with yourself and convince yourself the importance of maintaining a roster. 2) I want you to go out this Friday or Saturday night alone to a 3-star or above restaurant in your area. I want you to get dressed up and look your best. When you get there go and sit at the bar, order a drink or an appetizer. Keep an "inviting" body language and a smile. If a man approaches you be polite and engaging even if he isn't your type. Just enjoy the attention and practice being open. If he is your type, great. If you have no luck do not despair, be open to doing this exercise another weekend. We do not all strike out on our first hit.

Doing these two exercises will open you up to an abundance of men and the more men you have as suitors the more attractive you are to other men. So, get out of your comfort zone and get ready to attract the high-quality masculine man of your dreams.

Daily Assessment

1. Do you have any reservations about building a roster?

2. Will you go out this weekend and do this exercise?

3. If you did the exercise, how did It go? What did you learn?

4. What ways can you ensure that you are successful in maintaining your roster?

5. Are you committed to getting out and building your roster? If so, write the following statement in the lines below, "I am committed to the type of commitment I want and not to any one man. For this reason, I will actively keep at least three men on my roster at all times until I receive the relationship that I desire."

Additional Notes:

DAY

17

AFFIRMING YOUR FEMININITY

"It's the repetition of affirmations that leads to belief. And once that belief becomes a deep conviction, things begin to happen." -Claude Bristol

Today we will learn about affirming the feminine. We have gone into detail about how important it is to change your mind set in order to embrace your feminine essence. There is nothing that will change your mindset and beliefs more than affirmations. Affirmations are powerful, the more you do them the more they will change your perspectives and your deep-seated subconscious beliefs.

The subconscious is the part of your mind where all your perspectives, beliefs and views on life are held. Your subconscious is what propels you to behave in certain ways based on what it has learned and observed in your past conditioning.

You have programmed your subconscious with negative self-talk that has resulted in fear and worry in your relationships. This negative self-talk sank deep into your subconscious and caused you to act out of masculine energy, which has been detrimental to your connections with men. We need to replace that negative self-talk with powerful feminine affirmations.

Affirmations are positive phrases that represent something you want to be true about your present reality. Affirmations work best when you repeat them with emotion. You want to get in the feeling of each affirmation as you speak it. Without putting feeling behind your words your subconscious will not accept your reality as true and nothing will change for you. Convincing your subconscious is the key to changing your beliefs.

The subconscious learns through repetition, this is why you must repeat these phrases frequently in order to get them to be accepted by your subconscious. You will notice that the more you repeat these statements the easier it is to think, feel, and act in your feminine essence.

For today's assessment, I want you to choose 5 affirmations that resonate with you the most.

Remember to repeat them out loud to yourself daily, until you feel that your subconscious has fully accepted these as new truths about yourself. You can do these affirmations anywhere, doing anything. You will get the best results if you can do these looking at yourself in the mirror.

You are not stuck with just these affirmations. You can make up your own affirmations in addition to these and you can pick more than 5 from my list.

- I am a prize.
- I am feminine and graceful.
- I am feminine and open.
- I release control.
- I express my feelings freely.
- I trust my intuition.
- I put myself first.
- I deserve love.
- I love myself deeply.
- I trust the masculine.
- I am open to the masculine.
- I follow the masculine.
- I embrace vulnerability.
- I love my feelings.
- I relax.
- I own my feelings.

- I receive graciously.
- I love men.
- I am a goddess.
- I am attracting a high-quality masculine man to me now.

As you say some of these affirmations you may feel like they are complete and utter bullshit. This is normal. Your subconscious does not believe anything that you are saying. But if you keep it up your subconscious will start to believe the things that you are saying and changes will begin to happen.

Please be patient with yourself. Planting affirmations are like any new habit, you will see results if you keep it up but nothing will happen overnight.

Remember to do these affirmations daily. There are a lot of phone apps out there that can assist you in remembering to do these daily. You can even create alarms on your phone and have certain affirmations appear. Whatever seems easiest to you. Just make sure to commit to doing these affirmations daily.

Daily Assessment

1. What are the 5 affirmations you chose?

2. What feelings came up the first time you stated these affirmations?

3. I want you to practice these affirmations throughout the day, today, with strong emotion. How do you feel at the end of the day?

4. Are you committed to saying these affirmations until you believe them?

Additional Notes:

DAY

18

OWNING YOUR SHIT

"If you could kick the person in the pants most responsible for your trouble, you wouldn't sit for a month." - Theodore Roosevelt

Accountability is the only road to growth. When you stop blaming men for what has happened in your life you will be able to take ownership and change your life for the better.

Take a moment and think about all the failed relationships you've had. What is the common denominator? The common denominator in all of your failed relationship is ...YOU.

Many women I work with have never heard of feminine energy or maintaining a roster. They try to argue with me about these concepts I teach, giving justifications like, "What you are saying, feels like games.", "I do not have time to date multiple men." "There are no men in my town." "Having a roster is against my culture/religion/mom/society." These are statements of women who are stuck in the victim mentality and are not ready to own their stuff. Yet these women wonder why they have the same results over and over. Sigh…

You play yourself when you do not keep your options open. A woman who has a roster cannot be strung along because she is not able to give any one man too much of her attention. She cannot afford to put too much stock in one man and therefore he is not able to string her along or play her. She is not invested in the outcome. And that is the thing, being invested in an outcome is how you get strung along and played.

If you are playing the victim (admitting to being strung along or played) then you are admitting that you have surrendered your power. When you have a roster, you have options, and when you have options you have power. You can easily reject bad behavior without too much emotional strain.

A lot of women are practicing feminine energy but they are not practicing on several men. They are too focused on getting this one man using my 'tool', that they are in effect working against themselves. Most of these women are not in committed relationships and they are trying to use feminine energy as a method to get some type of commitment out of a certain man. This is the wrong use of feminine energy. Feminine energy is about taking your power back. You take your power back by committing to the type of relationship that you want, not to any one man.

I am currently working with a client, who first resisted me on this roster process. She fought me every time I told her that she was working against herself, by being exclusive with her man who after a few years still had not given her the proposal she was longing for. But after the fourth session of working with me she found that her man was talking to other women. She felt very angry and that he had 'strung her along.' I explained to her that he had not done anything wrong but she had in fact given her power over to him. If she had other options of men she would not have cared about what this man was doing or not doing. After this, she finally stopped resisting me on creating a roster. Now she is in the process of dating two men who are pursuing her passionately.

This is what happens when you date more than one man, your energy is very attractive to all the men around you. You are carefree and the opposite of needy. And men just flow to you.

Taking responsibility is about learning to love in a detached way so that you have no expectations of the outcome and cannot be hurt, strung along, or played.

When you feel like you got slighted in a relationship, it's because you held expectations that the other person did not sign up for. Men did not hurt you. You hurt yourself with your expectations, neediness, and low standards. I am not saying, that men have no fault but I am saying that men would only do what you allow.

When you take accountability, and realize that the common denominator in every failed relationship has been yourself you will be ready to find the love of your life. Because you will look at dating with a whole set of eyes that really see how you have to own your shit. This is when you will start to enjoy dating. You will begin to appreciate and live in the moment with men. You will be able to interact with men without anxiety, worry, and fear.

When you open yourself up to self-inventory and self-awareness you will begin to understand what type of man you want and therefore you will be able to recognize what type of man you do not want when they show up. That is one of the ways that you will be able to avoid wasting your time on the wrong men.

When you stop playing the victim and realize that no one is doing anything to you and that you are doing everything to yourself; you will be truly ready to attract the most amazing man you have ever met. You will be able to tune into your feminine energy around men and draw them to you.

No man can play you unless you offer yourself up on a platter to be played.

Do not try to control the situation or an outcome with a man. Do not try to fix it. Do not try to close the gap between you guys. Whatever a man is giving you either accept it or reject it. When you feel like you are not a priority to a man fall all the way back. Be hard to keep and easy to lose.

If you have this mentality and you take accountability you will never, ever be hurt. You can never be played if you pay attention to the actions of men. Men lie with their words but their actions are always truthful.

Having a roster will cause you to take self-inventory. It will cause you to look within and see how your energy; the vibe that you are giving out is affecting your interactions with men. It will give you the opportunity to practice your femininity and grow your self-worth. You will be able to get to this place where you will have gained back your power. When you have taken back your full power that is when no man can hurt you, no man can play you, and no man can string you along. You are unattached to the outcome and follow your heart at every moment. This is the power of femininity coupled with owning your shit.

Daily Assessment

1. Do you blame men when things go wrong?

2. Are you ready to take accountability for your love life?

3. What excuses have kept you in victim mode?

4. How have you been the source of your own pain in relationships?

Additional Notes:

DAY

19

VISION OR PERISH

"Where there is no vision, the people perish." - Proverbs 29:19 (the Bible)

In order to move from where you are to where you want to be, you must create a vision. A vision gets to the heart of why you want what you want. This book is helping you to become a more magnetic feminine woman who attracts high quality masculine men. Today's challenge is designed to bring the ideal masculine man that you desire to you.

With a vision, you are able to create momentum that will help you get to where your ultimate destination is: being in an amazing relationship!

In this way, you can go in the direction of your goal. You can get a man who is devoted to you if you believe you can.

If you do not have a vision, it will be hard for you to have boundaries and standards. People perish (fail) without vision because they are not able to distinguish the obstacles that will keep them away from their goals.

So, today you are going to do two exercises.

- Create a love vision statement.
- Create a love vision board.

In order to make sure you can identify the right man when he shows up, you must make a vision statement and vision board that will focus on your ideal man and marriage.

What is a love vision statement?

- What traits are you looking for in your future marriage?
- Why do you want this marriage?
- How do you want to feel in this marriage?

Here is an example:

"I want to have a marriage of love, security, and companionship. I want to wake up each day and feel excited because I get to share my life with my best friend."

Let's get into the vision board. A vision board is a board that you fill with images, words, affirmations, and phrases that represent goals that you want to achieve. In this instance, your goal is to manifest a marriage with a masculine, high quality man. It is important that you are specific when it comes to your vision statement and vision board.

You can make your vision board on an actual board or piece of construction paper, electronically on Pinterest, or a vision board app. Wherever you decide to create your vision board is not important but what is important is that your vision board always makes you feel good and represents what you want.

Vision boards are effective because they work actively with your subconscious and passively with your conscious mind to manifest what you desire.

A love vision board is a visual representation of your love vision statement.

Here are the guidelines for creating your vision board, assuming you are doing a traditional offline board (recommended):

- Put a picture of yourself in the center of the board. This will help your subconscious connect your desires with yourself.
- Underneath your picture write a gratitude statement, such as, "I am so happy and grateful now that…" Gratitude will always attract what you want.
- Use your love vision statement to get into the feelings of your ideal marriage. Also think of the traits you want in your future husband and include them on your board in the form of pictures and statements.
- Choose pictures that represent marriage, love, togetherness, and coupled fun. Be sure to include anything else that feels good to you.

Now, get into a comfortable position in a private area if you can and get ready to design your love vision board. Now take these images that you have found (online and offline) and place them wherever it feels good on your board. Do not glue or tape them down just yet. Feel free to position and reposition them until you have them exactly where you want them to be on the board. Now go ahead and glue or tape them down. Feel free to write statements, affirmations and any other written confirmation of your desires. If you want put, your love vision statement on your board.

Woolah, you are done! Hang your board where you will see it every day especially when you go to sleep and when you wake up. When you look at your vision board make sure to express gratitude and feel that you have already received your perfect marriage!

Now continue to work on your feminine energy and believe that your husband is on his way, because he is!

Daily Assessment

1. What is your love vision statement?

2. How did it feel creating your love vision statement and vision board?

3. Are you ready to manifest your ideal marriage?

4. You must have absolute faith that your amazing lover is on his way. I want you to write the following statement: "I am so grateful for my loving marriage with my ideal soul mate."

____

____

____

____

5. Do you feel inspired to take any action? If so, what?

____

____

____

____

Additional Notes:

DAY

20

BLOCKEDTTTT

"You don't ever have to feel guilty for removing toxic people from your life." - DaniellKoepke

When you are dating the 'block' button is your best friend. Becoming a more feminine woman is about holding true to your boundaries. You must learn to trust your intuition. When something does not feel good to you, express your feelings to your man. If you find yourself having to constantly repeat yourself... It's time for him to go.

Men who are dismissive, should be dismissed.

If a man is disregarding your feelings in major ways to you then it is your duty to respect your boundaries and standards and show him the door. Then add another man to the roster. Make sure you keep your roster full of high-quality men who show themselves to be husband material.

You have to make the decisions for what is okay for you in every moment. You have to get comfortable enough to listen to and feel your feelings and the sensations that are coming from your body.

When you set your boundaries, make sure that you do not compromise them for anyone. You have to do what is right for yourself. When it comes to finding 'the one' you have to be selfish with your affections in order to minimize heartbreak. For example, if a man on your roster disappears and reappears once every two weeks, you need to ask yourself, 'how does this make me feel? Is this a pattern? Is this the type of behavior I want in my future husband?' If you have mostly answered negative to these questions than it is time to block him and move on. Be on the lookout for another great high-quality man to add to your roster. You do not have time to teach men how to treat you; when a man shows you who he is believe him.

Now, I want to be clear; I am not saying you should block a man because he took an extra two hours to text you back on Thursday afternoon. I would say understand that you are dating and that just as you have a roster a man is possibly dating others as well. So be careful, don't have expectations but create boundaries and standards. Expectations are centered around men. Boundaries and standards are centered around you.

However, if you feel that something is a pattern and it's something that you just cannot deal with on a regular basis, then feel free to block him. I cannot tell you which scenarios deserve the benefit of the doubt and which scenarios you should just block. Listen to your inner guidance, listen to your feelings, and listen to your intuition they will tell you if something is not worth tolerating.

You have to make sure that you maintain a roster and you maintain a busy life so that you do not give any one man too much of your heart. You must remain unattached to the outcome and unattached to any man who isn't giving you the commitment that you desire. You also must set up your own individual boundaries that honor your femininity and self-worth. For example, you will not accept any last-minute dates, you want at least a 3-day notice, so that you can plan your week accordingly. So, that is your boundary. With this boundary in place you will be able to gauge when a man is not showing up for you in the way that you would like. If he invites you on a Friday night date on Thursday morning based on your boundary you have set in place you will turn that date down. If he continues to invite you on these dates last minute after you have expressed your boundaries to him he needs to be blocked. Remember a man who is dismissive to you needs to be dismissed.

You do not need to feel guilty or like you're being too harsh, men always put themselves first and they are not afraid to ghost and disappear on women who are not meeting their needs. I am not here to tell you to be like a man but what I am telling you is to not feel bad because a man will move you out of your life if you aren't meeting his needs without a second thought. So, you must be okay with putting your needs and your wants first. Do not worry about hurting someone's feelings or being rude. However, give people the same respect you would like. Respectfully state your feelings on the situation at hand and allow him an opportunity to correct the situation. If you find yourself having to continually speak on the same situation then you know it's time to remove him from the roster.

Keep your eyes on the prize. Do not be swayed by words that do not match actions. And do not be afraid to let someone go. When you let go what is not serving you, you are able to receive what will serve you.

Daily Assessment

1. Are you hesitant to block men? Why?

2. What are some situations you feel warrant a man getting blocked?

3. What are some situations you feel that do not warrant a man getting blocked?

4. How will you know when it's time to block?

5. How many chances are you willing to give a man before you remove him from your roster?

Additional Notes:

DAY 21

NEEDY AIN'T CUTE

"When a person goes into a relationship emotionally needy, they are not going to have discernment in choosing people." -Jennifer O'Neill

When you are not happy with who you are it is easy to become dependent upon a man for your happiness. You must develop inner happiness first before you can develop outer happiness. If you do not develop your own happiness you will easily become too attached to men. You will look to the men in your life to fulfill the void that is missing. That void is self-love. Without self-love, you cannot live a fulfilling, happy, and joyous life.

This is where neediness comes into play. A needy woman is a woman that's grasping for love outside of herself that she hasn't developed within herself. When you become needy you put too much emotional pressure on men and this causes them to want to back away from you. After all, how would you feel if someone else's entire source of happiness was you? It is not a good feeling.

Men are attracted to women who are happy, not women who are desperately seeking for someone to fill a void in their life. Here are some ways you can regain your inner happiness:

- Develop self-love and self-confidence. Begin to do things that make you feel vibrant: healthy diet, exercise, walks in nature, and whatever else makes you feel good. Begin to appreciate who you are as a person and all that you have to offer this world. Love yourself for who you are, flaws and all, but always be open to improvement.

- Develop boundaries and standards. Boundaries that you do not have will always be crossed. Learn to trust your intuition. Boundaries are established from your intuition. Standards are established based on your personal values. Once you have established boundaries and standards you will become a more confident and attractive woman.

- Find your passion. A passionate woman has a full life. It is fun and motivating. When you have found your passion, you exude inner joy. When you are full of genuine joy you are not in a place of neediness. You are in a profound state of self-love. As you enjoy life, you will see that you already have everything you need in order to be happy. This will cause you not to be needy.

- Work on your femininity. You become needy when you feel that your needs are not getting met. When you grow into a more feminine woman you will learn to trust your feelings. When you trust your feelings, you will remove yourself from any situation that is not meeting your needs.

Being needy is a major turnoff to men. Being needy lets a man know that he is the most important thing in your life. It lets him know that you do not have any options. It also feels like you are trying to pressure him into something that he isn't ready for. The attraction he has for you will start to dwindle. He will start to pull away and if you do not become self-aware you can find yourself being even more needy. Then the cycle will begin: his pulling away will cause your neediness, then your neediness will cause him to pull away until he pulls all the way away from you and leaves. Learn to cultivate your own life and passions so that you are fulfilled from the inside out.

Another way to avoid neediness is to stay realistic during your interactions with him. You stay realistic by mirroring him. When you are dating, mirroring looks like maintaining the same level of investment as him. If he only sees you once a week it means that he probably isn't ready to be in an exclusive situation. If he has not introduced you to anyone you, should not be thinking about introducing him to anyone. If he has not initiated conversations about a future you stay in the present. You do not get ahead of him.

The best way to mirror him is to always assume that he has a roster and since he has a roster you definitely should have a roster. Rosters will keep you grounded. Staying grounded means that you keep your energy around yourself. You do not let your emotions get to the point where you feel out of control. You do not blame or make anyone else responsible for your emotions. Keeping control of your emotions is how you avoid needy behavior.

The best thing for you to do is to care less so that he will care more. Own your inner goddess, and realize that you are your own source of love and fulfillment and then get out there and live happily ever after with yourself.

Daily Up Assessment

1. What does needy behavior look like to you?

____

____

____

____

2. What are some passions/hobbies that you have?

____

____

____

____

3. In your own words, explain why needy behavior is a turn off to men?

____

____

____

____

4. When you are feeling needy what is something you can go and do instead?

____

____

____

____

5. How will mirroring him keep you from being needy?

____

____

____

____

Additional Notes:

Bonus: Conversation Scripts

Emasculation Speech	Feminine Speech
"Why are you doing that?"	"I do not like ___. It makes me feel sad, mad, disappointed, weird, uncomfortable, etc.
"You need to stop doing…"	"I do not like ___. It makes me feel sad, mad, disappointed, weird, uncomfortable, etc.
"You never listen to me!"	"I do not like ___. It makes me feel sad, mad, disappointed, weird, uncomfortable, etc.
"Do this...do that."	"I do not like ___. It makes me feel sad, mad, disappointed, weird, uncomfortable, etc.
"Why didn't you call/text me?"	Nothing. Don't go there.
"I am not going there with you."	"I don't like that place. What do you think?"
"I want you to open my door, talk on the phone not text, I don't want to pick you up, etc."	"I am bit old-fashioned. I don't feel comfortable driving men, calling men, planning dates, etc."

Yay! You finished the book! I am so proud of you! I truly hope you gained a lot from this 21-day challenge. I hope you feel like a feminine magnet who is on her way to getting everything she desires in love and life! Feel free to come back and repeat the challenge as often as you need. You can also pick certain days that you felt you struggled with more or missed out in one way or the other.

Becoming a magnetically feminine woman will take a lot of practice. It will not be something you comprehend fully in under a month. It is something you will have to practice, practice, and practice. You have to move, breathe and eat femininity. It takes work. It takes dedication. But it is the most fulfilling journey. Everything about your love life will change. Here is what you need to do in order to get the commitment you desire -- the feminine way.

I believe in you!

A.S. Holcomb

Need More Writing Space?

Printed in Poland
by Amazon Fulfillment
Poland Sp. z o.o., Wrocław

36866652R00107